NAVY SHIPS
IN ACTION

Kay Jackson

PowerKiDS press.

New York

To Randi, who loves the ocean

Published in 2009 by The Rosen Publishing Group, Inc.
29 East 21st Street, New York, NY 10010

First Edition

Editor: Nicole Pristash
Book Design: Julio Gil
Photo Researcher: Jessica Gerweck

Photo Credits: Cover, pp. 5, 9, 10, 13, 14, 17, 18, 21 courtesy of the U.S. Navy; p. 6 © Getty Images.

Library of Congress Cataloging-in-Publication Data

Jackson, Kay, 1959-
  Navy ships in action / Kay Jackson. — 1st ed.
      p. cm. — (Amazing military vehicles)
  Includes index.
  ISBN 978-1-4358-2750-9 (library binding) — ISBN 978-1-4358-3160-5 (pbk.)
ISBN 978-1-4358-3166-7 (6-pack)
  1. Warships—United States—Juvenile literature. 2. United States. Navy—Juvenile literature. I. Title.
  VA58.4.J34 2009
  623.825—dc22
                            2008034412

Manufactured in the United States of America

CONTENTS

Navy Ships Across the World

On a stormy sea, ocean waves taller than two-story buildings crash into a huge ship. The ship's lights disappear and come back into view as the ship rises and falls with the waves. Even in storms like this, jets take off and land on the ship.

The lights of other ships flash through the rain. Some of these ships carry troops, and others carry **fuel** and food. One thing connects these ships, though. All of these ships are part of the U.S. Navy. Navy ships bring the force of the U.S. military around the world.

Navy ships, like the ones shown here, are powerful and built to be strong. These ships are ready for the Navy to use anytime and anywhere.

This painting shows the USS *Constitution* (right) fighting with an enemy ship. The *Constitution* was one of the U.S. Navy's first warships. Its nickname is Old Ironsides.

From Wood to High Technology

The U.S. Navy has a rich past. Navy ships were first used during the Revolutionary War, in the eighteenth century. These wooden ships stood taller than many buildings at the time. Then, in the late 1800s, metal took the place of wood, and engines took the place of sails. By World War II, Navy ships carried huge guns that were 16 inches (406 mm) wide.

Today's ships have a lot of high **technology**. Modern ships have **sonar** that can find objects hundreds of feet (m) deep in the water. New Navy ships will be harder for the enemy to find.

Ships of Steel

A Navy ship is a large ship built to withstand huge waves. Most Navy ships are made of steel, which is a hard metal. A steel body allows the ship to stand up to the powerful sea.

Each Navy ship has a bridge. On the bridge, the captain of the ship uses a wheel to push the ship's rudder from side to side. A rudder is an underwater blade that **steers** a ship.

Inside the ship is an engine room. The engines turn long tubes that have **propellers**. The propellers spin to push the ship through the water.

Here a Navy crew member is shown on the bridge of the USS *Gladiator*. He is studying charts so he can help decide which way his ship should go.

In this picture, the USNS *Guadalupe* (right) is refueling the USS *Kitty Hawk*, an aircraft carrier, out at sea. Navy ships work together as part of a team.

Kinds of Navy Ships

The U.S. Navy has planes, helicopters, and trucks, as the Army and the Marines do. The Navy even has military bases on land. However, most of the Navy's work is done at sea.

Navy ships come in all sizes, and they have many different jobs. Most Navy ships are built to fire **missiles** and rockets at the enemy. Some Navy ships look for mines and **submarines**. The Navy also has ships that are like floating stores. These ships take food, fuel, mail, and engine parts to other ships. The Navy, though, is best known for its giant aircraft carriers.

Aircraft Carriers

Aircraft carriers are floating airports. Carriers have flat tops from which military planes land and take off. The top is as long as three football fields! On a busy day, a plane takes off or lands every 5 minutes. Carriers help keep peace in troubled places and bring the U.S. military to different countries.

Aircraft carriers are like small cities. They have movie theaters, hospitals, and gyms. A crew on a carrier makes more than 18,000 meals each day. Carriers carry around 85 jets, and they can travel over 30,000 miles (48,280 km) without stopping for fuel!

These Navy planes are flying over the USS *Kitty Hawk*. On Navy carriers, two planes can take off and one plane can land every 37 seconds during daylight!

This MK45 Mod 4 gun on the USS *Winston S. Churchill*, a Navy destroyer, is being fired. This gun can fire at an enemy more than 60 miles (97 km) away.

Destroyers

Navy destroyers are ships that are built to destroy enemy boats. Destroyers have guns and missiles to shoot down planes. They also carry **torpedoes** to sink enemy submarines and ships. Another important job for a destroyer is to keep larger Navy ships safe. Destroyers often sail in groups made up of aircraft carriers, submarines, and other destroyers.

Destroyers have **radar** that warns the crew when the enemy is close by. Destroyers are very fast, too. They do not have a lot of heavy armor on them. Armor is a hard cover put over something to keep it safe.

The Gator Navy

The Navy has a group of ships that is nicknamed the Gator Navy. These ships are amphibious ships. An amphibious ship can work on land and in the water, just as an alligator can. Amphibious ships move troops, trucks, and supplies from the sea onto land.

An amphibious **assault** ship is **similar** to a small aircraft carrier. Helicopters take off from its top deck, and boats called landing craft take off from a large deck below. Fans blow air under these landing craft and lift them up. This allows the boats to float above the water and the sand.

This is the USS *Essex*, an amphibious assault ship. This ship can carry around 30 helicopters, several landing craft, and around 1,800 troops at sea.

This Seahawk helicopter is lifting supplies from the USNS *Bridge*, a support ship. The helicopter will then take the supplies to a nearby aircraft carrier.

Supplying the Navy

Combat support ships carry supplies to other Navy ships and planes while they are on the ocean. This is so that the other ships do not have to go back to land to get their supplies. Support ships must be fast so they can keep up with the other ships.

Combat support ships can carry nearly 2 million gallons (8 million l) of fuel for other ships, smaller boats, and jet planes. Support ships can also store 2,000 tons (1,814 t) of guns and missiles, 500 tons (454 t) of dry food, and 250 tons (227 t) of cold food.

Working on Ships

There are hundreds of jobs on a Navy ship. Some sailors learn to use sonar to hear sounds under the sea. These sailors listen for torpedoes, submarines, other ships, and even whales. Many sailors work on the engines, and others use maps and computers to find their way. There are crew members in the ship's hospital who take care of the sick and wounded sailors. Officers help run the ship, and the captain is in charge of everyone.

Sailors and officers train for their jobs at Navy schools. Navy crews train together so they learn to work as a team.

eing a good crew member means taking care of your ship and helping others.
hese Navy crew members are working together to move a heavy chain.

Navy Ships of Tomorrow

To make sure Navy ships can continue to do new jobs, new ships are being made. For example, the Zumwalt destroyer will be very hard to find on an enemy's radar. It will also be able to support troops on land as well as ships on the water.

The U.S. Navy's ships sail thousands of miles (km) each year. They go to other countries to help fight wars, and they bring supplies, clean water, and food to troops and the needy. Navy ships are important tools of the U.S. Navy, and they will be used for a long time.

Glossary

ssault (eh-SOLT) An attack.

ombat (KOM-bat) A battle or a fight.

uel (FYOOL) Something used to make warmth or power.

missiles (MIH-sulz) Objects that are shot at something far away.

ropellers (pruh-PEL-erz) Paddlelike parts on an object that spin to move the object forward.

adar (RAY-dahr) A way of finding objects using radio waves.

imilar (SIH-muh-ler) Almost the same as.

onar (SOH-nahr) A way of finding objects using sound waves.

teers (STEERS) Guides something's path.

ubmarines (SUB-muh-reenz) Ships that are made to travel underwater.

upport (suh-PORT) Giving necessities.

echnology (tek-NAH-luh-jee) The way people do something and the tools they use to do it.

orpedoes (tor-PEE-dohz) Underwater missiles that blow up when they hit something.

Index

A
aircraft carrier(s), 11–12, 15–16

F
food, 4, 11, 19, 22
fuel, 4, 11–12, 19

J
jets, 4, 12

M
missiles, 11, 15, 19

P
planes, 11–12, 15, 19
propellers, 8

R
radar, 15, 22
rudder, 8

S
sea, 4, 11, 16, 20
sonar, 7, 20
submarines, 11, 15, 20
supplies, 16, 19, 22

T
technology, 7
torpedoes, 15, 20
troops, 4, 16, 22

U
U.S. military, 4, 12
U.S. Navy, 4, 7, 11, 16, 22

V
view, 4

Web Sites

Due to the changing nature of Internet links, PowerKids Press has developed an online list of Web sites related to the subject of this book. This site is updated regularly. Please use this link to access the list:

www.powerkidslinks.com/amv/ships/